FROM CANADA🍁 TO THE WORLD

PROVEN EXPORT STRATEGIES FOR CANADIAN MANUFACTURERS

BY **PEYMAN CHALABI**

Serial Number: P2546120257
Title: From Canada to the World
Sub-title: Proven Export Strategies for Canadian Manufacturers
Author: Peyman Chalabi
Layout Designer: Monika Davis
ISBN: 978-1-77892-190-2
Subject: Business / Export Strategy
Format: Paperback, (Royal size)
Pages Count: 112 pages
Publication Date: May 2025
Publisher: Kidsocado Publishing House

Kidsocado Publishing House
Vancouver, Canada

Phone: +1 (236) 333-7248
WhatsApp: +1 (236) 333-7248
Email: info@kidsocado.com
Website: https://kidsocado.com
Address: 2100-1055 West Georgia St,
Vancouver, BC V6E 3P3, Canada

CONTENTS

ACKNOWLEDGMENT

First and foremost, I would like to express my deepest gratitude to my wife, Mahmonir—my partner in life and business for the past 13 years. From the very first day of our marriage, we have walked every step of this journey together—building dreams, facing challenges, and growing through every twist and turn.

Our shared path has not always been easy. Especially after moving to Canada, we faced countless hurdles in building our business from the ground up in a new country. There were moments of doubt, frustration, and exhaustion—but through it all, your unwavering support, strength, and belief in our vision never faded.

You have been more than just a partner—you have been my anchor, my motivator, my greatest source of courage, and my best friend. Without your dedication, patience, and sacrifices, this book would never have come to life.

This is not just a milestone for me—it's our shared victory. Thank you for everything you are, and for always standing by me with love and resilience.

PREFACE

Exporting has long been a cornerstone of Canada's economic strength. With a wealth of natural resources, advanced manufacturing capabilities, and a reputation for quality, Canadian businesses are well-positioned to compete on the global stage. Yet, for many manufacturers, expanding into international markets can be complex, fraught with regulatory challenges, logistical hurdles, and shifting trade policies. This book was written to bridge the gap between ambition and execution, providing a structured roadmap for Canadian manufacturers looking to expand their global reach.

Over the years, I have worked with numerous businesses striving to navigate the intricacies of export development. I have witnessed firsthand the challenges they face—ranging from compliance with international standards to the complexities of supply chain management. However, I have also seen the transformative power of a well-executed export strategy, one that not only drives revenue growth but also enhances the resilience of businesses in an increasingly competitive world.

This book is designed to be a practical guide, equipping manufacturers with the knowledge and tools needed to succeed in international markets. Each chapter delves into crucial aspects of export development, from identifying new market opportunities to leveraging government support programs. Throughout the book, real-world examples, data-driven insights, and actionable strategies will help demystify the export process, enabling businesses to confidently step onto the global stage.

Whether you are a seasoned manufacturer looking to refine your export strategy or a business just beginning to explore international markets, this book will serve as a valuable resource. My goal is to provide you with the clarity and confidence needed to seize global opportunities and drive sustainable growth.

Thank you for embarking on this journey with me. I hope this book inspires and empowers you to take your business beyond borders, unlocking new levels of success in the global marketplace.

Peyman Chalabi

INTRODUCTION

Global markets present a vast landscape of opportunities for Canadian manufacturers. As the world becomes increasingly interconnected, businesses that tap into international trade can unlock new revenue streams, achieve greater brand recognition, and gain a competitive edge. However, expanding beyond domestic borders comes with its own set of challenges—navigating trade regulations, understanding cultural differences, managing supply chains, and securing financing for global operations. This book serves as a roadmap to help Canadian manufacturers successfully expand into international markets.

With Canada's strong foundation in manufacturing and an extensive network of trade agreements, businesses have unprecedented access to foreign markets. Yet, many manufacturers hesitate to expand due to uncertainty about the process, concerns about risks, or lack of knowledge about available resources. **From Canada To The World: Proven Export Strategies for Canadian Manufacturers** provides practical guidance on every step of the export journey, from assessing readiness to executing successful market entry strategies.

This book is designed for business owners, executives, and decision-makers in the manufacturing industry who want to grow beyond Canada's borders. Whether you are a small manufacturer taking your first steps into exporting or an established company looking to enhance your international presence, you will find actionable insights, real-world examples, and proven strategies to help you succeed.

By the end of this book, you will have a clear understanding of how to identify global opportunities, develop a strategic export plan, navigate trade regulations, optimize logistics, and build long-term relationships with international customers.

Exporting is not just about selling products abroad—it's about sustainable growth, innovation, and positioning your business for long-term success in the global marketplace.

Are you ready to take your manufacturing business beyond borders? Let's begin the journey.

CHAPTER 1
UNDERSTANDING GLOBAL MARKET OPPORTUNITIES

Highlights of this Chapter

- ☑ The Importance of Exporting for Canadian Manufacturers
- ☑ The Role of Market Research in Export Development
- ☑ Key Markets for Canadian Manufacturers
- ☑ Case Study: A Canadian Manufacturer's Global Expansion
- ☑ Tools and Resources for Market Research
- ☑ Actionable Steps for Manufacturers
- ☑ Summary

The Importance of Exporting for Canadian Manufacturers

Canada's manufacturing sector has long been a driving force in the national economy. However, as global markets evolve and competition intensifies, businesses must expand beyond domestic borders to achieve sustainable growth. Exporting allows Canadian manufacturers to tap into new revenue streams, mitigate risks associated with local market fluctuations, and build resilience against economic downturns.

The Role of Market Research in Export Development

Before entering foreign markets, Canadian manufacturers must conduct thorough market research to identify opportunities and mitigate risks. This includes:

1. **Assessing Demand:**

   a. Understanding the demand for Canadian products in different countries.

   b. Analyzing trade data and consumer preferences.

2. **Evaluating Competition:**

   a. Identifying key competitors and their market positioning.

   b. Assessing pricing strategies, product differentiation, and market share.

3. **Understanding Economic and Political Conditions:**

   a. Examining economic stability, currency fluctuations, and trade barriers.

   b. Analyzing government policies, tax structures, and business regulations.

Key Markets for Canadian Manufacturers

1. United States – Canada's Largest Trading Partner

- Benefits from the **Canada-United States-Mexico Agreement (CUSMA)**.

- Similar business culture and consumer preferences.

- Strong demand for Canadian industrial and consumer goods.

2. European Union – Expanding Opportunities Through CETA

- The **Comprehensive Economic and Trade Agreement (CETA)** eliminates tariffs on most goods.

- High demand for high-quality Canadian machinery, aerospace, and agricultural products.

- Requires compliance with stringent EU regulations and certifications.

3. Asia-Pacific – Rapidly Growing Markets

- **China, Japan, South Korea, and India** are key importers of Canadian goods.

- The **Comprehensive and Progressive Agreement for Trans-Pacific Partnership (CPTPP)** provides preferential market access.

- Demand for Canadian technology, raw materials, and agri-food products is rising.

4. Latin America and Emerging Markets

- Countries like **Mexico, Brazil, and Chile** offer expanding opportunities.

- Growing middle-class populations increase demand for Canadian manufactured goods.

- Establishing partnerships and distribution networks is key to success.

Case Study: A Canadian Manufacturer's Global Expansion

XYZ Manufacturing, a Toronto-based auto parts manufacturer, sought to expand beyond Canada.

Through market research, they identified Germany as a high-potential market due to its automotive industry. By leveraging **CETA**, they:

- Eliminated 98% of tariffs on their products.

- Secured partnerships with European distributors.

- Met EU regulatory standards to ensure smooth market entry.

Within **two years**, XYZ Manufacturing increased export revenue by **35%**, demonstrating the power of strategic market selection and research.

Tools and Resources for Market Research

To support their export strategy, manufacturers can leverage the following resources:

1. **Government Programs:** Export Development Canada (EDC), Trade

Commissioner Service (TCS), and Business Development Canada (BDC).

2. **Market Intelligence Reports:** Provided by the World Bank, Statistics Canada, and industry associations.

3. **Trade Shows and Business Forums:** Participating in international exhibitions to network with potential buyers.

Actionable Steps for Manufacturers

1. **Conduct a Market Feasibility Study:** Identify target regions based on demand, competition, and trade agreements.

2. **Develop a Competitor Analysis Report:** Understand key players in the industry and how to differentiate your product.

3. **Build a Market Entry Plan:** Define pricing, distribution, and promotional strategies for new markets.

4. **Engage with Trade Experts:** Consult export advisors and leverage government support programs.

Summary

Understanding global market opportunities is the first step toward successful export development.

With thorough research, strategic planning, and leveraging trade agreements, Canadian manufacturers can position themselves for sustained international growth.

CHAPTER 2

DEVELOPING AN EFFECTIVE EXPORT STRATEGY

Highlights of this Chapter:

- ☑ Introduction: Why a Strategy Matters
- ☑ Key Elements of a Successful Export Strategy
- ☑ Case Study: How ABC Manufacturing Successfully Entered the U.S. Market
- ☑ Actionable Steps for Manufacturers
- ☑ Summary

Introduction: Why a Strategy Matters

Expanding into global markets without a clear export strategy is like setting sail without a map. Canadian manufacturers must develop a well-structured plan to ensure smooth entry, compliance, and long-term success in foreign markets. A strong export strategy helps businesses mitigate risks, maximize opportunities, and allocate resources effectively.

Key Elements of a Successful Export Strategy

1. Defining Business Objectives

    a. Establish clear short-term and long-term export goals.

    b. Determine key performance indicators (KPIs) such as revenue growth, market penetration, and brand recognition.

2. Selecting the Right Markets

a. Conduct market research to assess demand, competition, and economic stability.

b. Prioritize countries with trade agreements that provide Canadian manufacturers with tariff benefits.

3. **Understanding Trade Regulations and Compliance**

a. Familiarize yourself with destination country regulations, product standards, and customs requirements.

b. Work with trade specialists to avoid legal issues and ensure smooth clearance of goods.

4. **Pricing and Cost Considerations**

a. Determine the right pricing strategy by factoring in production costs, tariffs, transportation, and local market expectations.

b. Analyze competitors' pricing models and assess price elasticity in different regions.

5. **Distribution and Logistics Planning**

   a. Choose the right distribution model: direct sales, agents, distributors, or joint ventures.

   b. Plan for efficient logistics, including warehousing, shipping, and customs clearance.

6. **Marketing and Branding for International Markets**

   a. Adapt branding and marketing messages to suit local cultures and consumer behaviors.

   b. Leverage digital marketing, e-commerce, and trade shows to build brand awareness globally.

7. **Financing and Risk Management**

   a. Identify funding sources such as government grants, export financing, and private investors.

   b. Develop strategies to manage currency fluctuations, credit risks, and potential payment delays.

Case Study: How ABC Manufacturing Successfully Entered the U.S. Market

ABC Manufacturing, a Vancouver-based machinery manufacturer, developed an export strategy to enter the U.S. market. They:

- Conducted competitor analysis and identified niche opportunities.

- Partnered with a local distributor to streamline operations.

- Took advantage of **CUSMA (Canada-United States-Mexico Agreement)** to reduce tariffs.

- Implemented a U.S.-focused digital marketing campaign.

Within **18 months**, they expanded their client base by **40%**, proving the effectiveness of a well-planned export strategy.

Actionable Steps for Manufacturers

1. **Draft an Export Business Plan:** Outline target markets, pricing strategies, and distribution channels.

2. **Seek Expert Advice:** Work with trade consultants and export development agencies.

3. **Utilize Government Resources:** Leverage support from **Export Development Canada (EDC)** and **Trade Commissioner Service (TCS).**

4. **Pilot a Test Market:** Launch products in a single international market before scaling globally.

Summary

A robust export strategy is the foundation for long-term success in global markets. By carefully planning market entry, pricing, logistics, and marketing, Canadian manufacturers can increase their competitiveness and achieve sustainable growth.

CHAPTER 3
NAVIGATING INTERNATIONAL TRADE REGULATIONS

Highlights of this Chapter

- ☑ Introduction: The Importance of Regulatory Compliance
- ☑ Understanding Trade Agreements and Their Impact
- ☑ Key Trade Regulations Affecting Canadian Manufacturers
- ☑ Case Study: Overcoming Trade Barriers in Europe
- ☑ Actionable Steps for Manufacturers
- ☑ Summary

Introduction: The Importance of Regulatory Compliance

International trade regulations can be complex and vary significantly from one country to another. For Canadian manufacturers looking to expand globally, understanding and complying with these regulations is critical to avoiding legal issues, minimizing delays, and ensuring smooth market entry. Non-compliance can result in penalties, shipment refusals, and reputational damage.

Understanding Trade Agreements and Their Impact

Canada has several trade agreements that provide Canadian manufacturers with reduced tariffs, preferential market access, and regulatory alignment. The table below outlines some of the most significant trade agreements and their benefits.

Table 3.1: Key Trade Agreements and Benefits for Canadian Manufacturers

Trade Agreement	Member Countries	Key Benefits
CUSMA (Canada-United States-Mexico Agreement)	Canada, U.S., Mexico	Tariff-free trade on most goods, stronger IP protection, streamlined customs procedures
CETA (Comprehensive Economic and Trade Agreement)	Canada, EU	Eliminates tariffs, faster customs clearance, regulatory cooperation
CPTPP (Comprehensive and Progressive Agreement for Trans-Pacific Partnership)	Canada, 11 Asia-Pacific countries	Eliminates 95% of tariffs, enhances labor mobility, strengthens investor protections

Key Trade Regulations Affecting Canadian Manufacturers:

1. Tariffs and Duties

   a. Understanding applicable tariffs in target markets.

   b. Utilizing trade agreements to minimize costs.

   c. Working with customs brokers to streamline the process.

2. Product Standards and Certifications

a. Ensuring compliance with safety and quality standards (e.g., CE Marking for the EU, FDA regulations for the U.S.).

b. Obtaining necessary certifications before shipping goods.

c. Adapting packaging and labeling to meet country-specific requirements.

3. Customs Procedures and Documentation

a. Preparing export documentation, including invoices, certificates of origin, and shipping   manifests.

b. Understanding import/export restrictions and prohibited goods.

c. Leveraging digital trade platforms to expedite processing.

The following flowchart illustrates the customs clearance process for Canadian exports.

Figure 3.1: Customs Clearance Process for Canadian Manufacturers

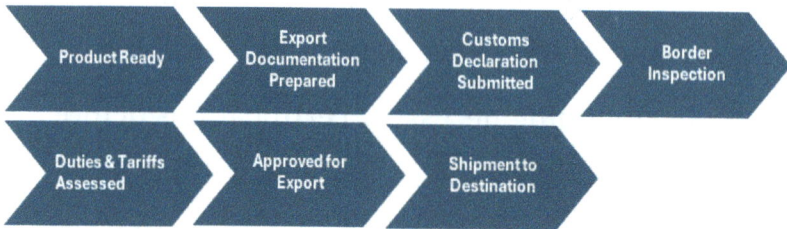

The Impact of Trade Agreements on Canadian Exports

The graph below illustrates the impact of trade agreements on Canadian exports over the past decade. A noticeable increase in exports occurred after signing agreements like CETA and CPTPP.

Figure 3.2: Growth of Canadian Exports Post-Trade Agreements (2010–2023)

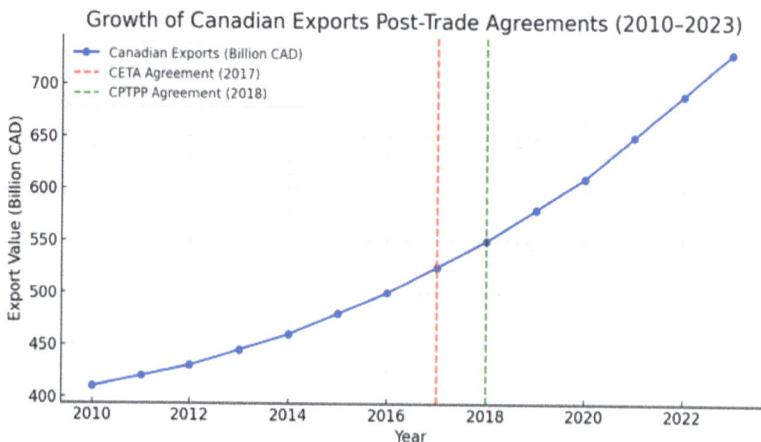

Growth of Canadian Exports Post-Trade Agreements (2010-2023)

Case Study: Overcoming Trade Barriers in Europe

A Canadian manufacturer specializing in medical devices faced regulatory hurdles when entering the EU market. To comply with **CE marking** requirements, they:

- Partnered with a local compliance consultant.
- Adjusted product designs to meet European safety standards.
- Registered with the European Medicines Agency for faster approval.

As a result, they gained **market access within 12 months** and increased export revenue by **30%**.

Actionable Steps for Manufacturers:

1. **Conduct a Trade Compliance Audit:** Identify key regulatory requirements in target markets.

2. **Work with Export Consultants:** Engage with trade compliance experts to navigate regulations.

3. **Register for Required Certifications:** Ensure all products meet country-specific standards.

4. **Utilize Government Support:** Leverage services from the **Canadian Border Services Agency (CBSA)** and **Export Development Canada (EDC).**

Summary

Navigating international trade regulations is a critical step in the export journey. By understanding trade agreements, tariffs, product standards, and compliance requirements, Canadian manufacturers can avoid costly delays and successfully expand into global markets.

CHAPTER 4

BUILDING STRONG INTERNATIONAL PARTNERSHIPS

Highlights of this Chapter

Introduction: The Power of Strategic Partnerships

Expanding into global markets requires more than just a strong product—it demands **strategic international partnerships** that facilitate smooth market entry, operational efficiency, and long-term success. Whether partnering with distributors, suppliers, or local businesses, **collaborative efforts can reduce risks, enhance credibility, and accelerate market penetration.**

Understanding the Different Types of International Partnerships

Canadian manufacturers can form various types of partnerships depending on their business goals and target markets. Some of the most effective partnerships include:

1. Distributorship Agreements

- **Description:** Working with local distributors who sell and promote products in a foreign market.

- **Benefits:** Access to existing distribution networks, market knowledge, and reduced logistical challenges.

- **Challenges:** Dependency on third parties, profit-sharing, and possible brand misrepresentation.

2. Joint Ventures

- **Description:** A legal business arrangement where two companies share ownership and resources to enter a market.

- **Benefits:** Shared financial risk, better local market acceptance, and combined expertise.

- **Challenges:** Complex legal structures, cultural differences, and decision-making conflicts.

3. Strategic Alliances

- **Description:** A cooperative agreement between two companies to pursue a common goal without forming a new entity.

- **Benefits:** Cost-effective collaboration, flexibility, and access to resources.

- **Challenges:** No legal binding, risk of knowledge sharing with competitors.

4. Licensing Agreements

- **Description:** Allowing foreign businesses to produce and sell products under a licensing agreement.

- **Benefits:** Low-cost market entry, passive income streams, and expanded brand presence.

- **Challenges:** Loss of control over product quality and brand representation.

Key Factors for Successful International Partnerships

To ensure a successful collaboration, manufacturers should consider the following:

1. Cultural and Business Compatibility

- Understand the local culture, business etiquette, and consumer behavior.

- Ensure partners align with your company's values and long-term vision.

2. Legal and Contractual Clarity

- Establish clear contracts that outline roles, responsibilities, revenue sharing, and dispute resolution mechanisms.

- Seek legal counsel to ensure compliance with international trade laws.

3. Trust and Transparency

- Conduct due diligence on potential partners.

- Establish transparent communication and accountability measures.

4. Market Research and Feasibility Studies

- Evaluate the target market's demand, regulatory requirements, and competitive landscape.

- Utilize government trade agencies like **Export Development Canada (EDC)** for research support.

Case Study: A Successful Partnership in Asia
A Canadian electronics manufacturer successfully entered the **Japanese market** through a strategic alliance with a local distributor. Here's how they did it:

1. Conducted extensive **market research** on Japanese consumer electronics trends.

2. Partnered with a **well-established Japanese distributor** with existing retail networks.

3. Adapted product features and packaging to meet **Japanese quality and branding standards.**

4. Implemented a joint **marketing and pricing strategy** for competitive positioning.

5. Achieved **35% market penetration** in the first two years, exceeding revenue projections.

Graph: The Impact of Partnerships on Export Success

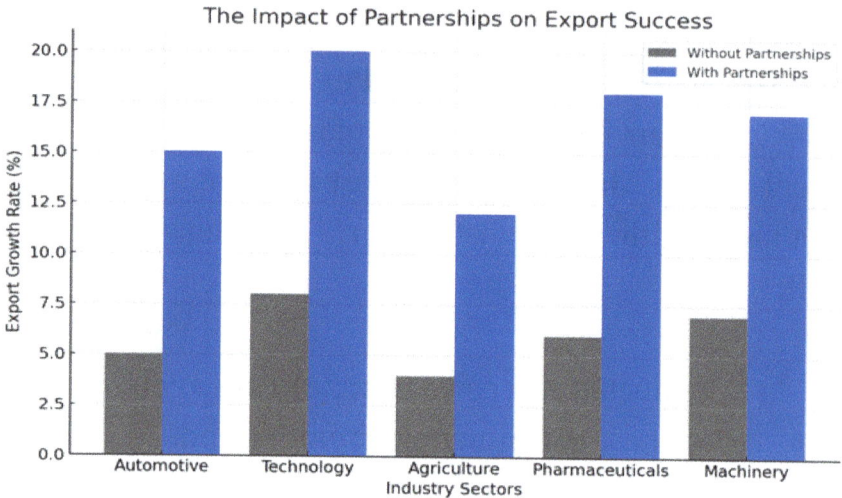

The Impact of Partnerships on Export Success

International partnerships and trade agreements have been shown to significantly enhance export growth across various sectors. For instance, businesses engaged in international trade are approximately 20% more productive than those operating solely domestically. Moreover, exporters have been observed to grow at nearly double the rate of non-exporting businesses. (https://impact. economist.com/perspectives/strategy-leadership/ growth-amid-uncertainty-insights-international-export-success?utm_source=chatgpt.com)

To illustrate this impact, consider the case of the United Arab Emirates (UAE). In 2024, the UAE's non-oil trade reached a record 3 trillion dirhams (approximately $817 billion), marking a 14.6% increase from the previous year. This growth was largely attributed to the UAE's strategy of diversifying its economy through comprehensive economic partnership agreements with countries such as India, Indonesia, Israel, and Turkey. (https://www. reuters.com/world/middle-east/uae-leans-trade-deals-growth-non-oil-trade-jumps-15-2024-2025-02-05/?utm_source=chatgpt.com)

Similarly, the implementation of free trade agreements (FTAs) has been linked to increased trade flows between member countries by lowering import barriers and opening markets. For example, more than half of U.S. agricultural imports come from FTA partners, particularly low- and middle-income countries.

These examples underscore the positive correlation between international partnerships and export growth. By collaborating with foreign entities and entering into trade agreements, countries and businesses can access new markets, enhance productivity, and achieve substantial economic growth.

Government Support for International Partnerships

The **Canadian Trade Commissioner Service (TCS)** and **Export Development Canada (EDC)** offer valuable resources to help manufacturers establish international partnerships. These include:

- **Market intelligence reports**
- **Business matchmaking services**
- **Financial support for partnership development**
- **Legal advisory services**

Actionable Steps for Manufacturers

1. **Identify potential partners** through trade associations, business networking events, and government resources.

2. **Perform due diligence** on potential partners' financial stability, reputation, and market influence.

3. **Negotiate agreements** that define clear expectations, responsibilities, and revenue-sharing models.

4. **Establish regular performance evaluations** to measure the partnership's success and make improvements.

5. **Stay adaptable** to evolving market trends and be open to adjusting partnership strategies.

Summary

Building strong international partnerships is essential for Canadian manufacturers looking to expand globally. By selecting the right type of collaboration, conducting thorough research, and utilizing available government resources, businesses can achieve long-term success in international markets.

CHAPTER 5

NAVIGATING GOVERNMENT'S POLICIES, INCENTIVES, AND COMPLIANCE FOR EXPORT SUCCESS

Highlights of this Chapter

- ☑ Introduction
- ☑ Government Policies Supporting Export Growth
- ☑ Analytical Insights
- ☑ Step-by-Step Export Funding Process
- ☑ Key Insights
- ☑ International Export Compliance Checklist
- ☑ Case Study: A Manufacturer's Success with Government Support
- ☑ Key Observations
- ☑ Conclusion

Introduction

Exporting requires more than just identifying international markets—it involves navigating a complex web of government policies, financial incentives, and compliance regulations. Canadian manufacturers must understand these aspects to maximize opportunities while ensuring legal and regulatory adherence. This chapter provides an in-depth look at essential government policies, funding options, and compliance requirements that impact exports.

1. Government Policies Supporting Export Growth

The Canadian government has implemented numerous policies to support manufacturers looking to expand internationally. Some of the key policy areas include:

1.1 Free Trade Agreements (FTAs)

Canada is a member of several free trade agreements that reduce tariffs, eliminate trade barriers, and create new opportunities for manufacturers. Some of the most impactful agreements include:

Free Trade Agreement	Key Benefits
CUSMA (Canada-United (States-Mexico Agreement	Tariff-free access to North American markets, regulatory alignment
CETA (Comprehensive Economic and Trade Agree-(ment	Expanded opportunities for exports to Europe, reduced tariffs
CPTPP (Comprehensive and Progressive Agreement for (Trans-Pacific Partnership	Opens doors to Asian and Pacific markets, competitive advantages

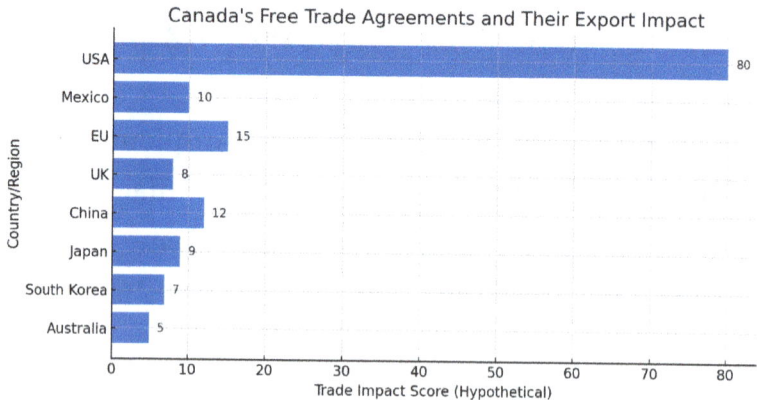

Canada's Free Trade Agreements and Their Export Impact

Country/Region	Trade Impact Score (Hypothetical)
USA	80
Mexico	10
EU	15
UK	8
China	12
Japan	9
South Korea	7
Australia	5

Analytical Insights:

1. **Strong Dependence on the US** – Canada's trade relationship with the US remains dominant, contributing to about 80% of its total export impact due to the USMCA agreement.

2. **Growing Opportunities in the EU & UK** – The CETA (Comprehensive Economic and Trade Agreement) and the UK-Canada Trade Continuity Agreement offer expanding opportunities in Europe.

3. **Asia-Pacific Growth** – Agreements like CPTPP (Comprehensive and Progressive Agreement for Trans-Pacific Partnership) help Canadian exporters access Japan, South Korea, and Australia, although these markets still have room for expansion.

4. **China as an Emerging Partner** – Despite trade tensions, China remains an important export market, particularly for natural resources and agriculture.

1.2 Export Development Policies

The federal and provincial governments have established several policies to encourage exports:

- **Innovation and Skills Plan:** Supports research, development, and innovation.

- **Global Markets Action Plan:** Aligns trade policies with business needs.

- **Canadian Trade Commissioner Service (TCS):** Provides market intelligence and networking opportunities.

2. Financial Incentives and Funding for Exporters

Many government agencies and financial institutions offer funding, grants, and financial support to Canadian manufacturers seeking to export.

2.1 Key Export Funding Programs

Funding Program	Description
CanExport Program	Provides funding to SMEs for export market development.
Export Development Canada (EDC) Financing	Offers loans, insurance, and financial tools for international growth.
Industrial Research Assistance Program (IRAP)	Funds innovation to improve export potential.
Scientific Research and Experimental Development (SR&ED) Program	Provides tax credits for R&D initiatives supporting export growth.

Step-by-Step Export Funding Process

1. **Identify Funding Opportunities** → Research government programs such as CanExport, Export Development Canada (EDC) financing, or trade mission grants.

2. **Assess Eligibility** → Review program requirements related to industry, export destination, and business size.

3. **Prepare Documentation** → Gather financial statements, business plans, and market entry strategies.

4. **Submit Application** → Fill out application forms and submit them through the respective government portal.

5. **Approval & Review** → Government agencies evaluate applications based on export potential and compliance.

6. **Funding Allocation** → Approved businesses receive funding for export-related activities like trade shows, marketing, or logistics.

7. **Reporting & Compliance** → Submit periodic reports on fund utilization and export performance.

Government Export Funding Application Process

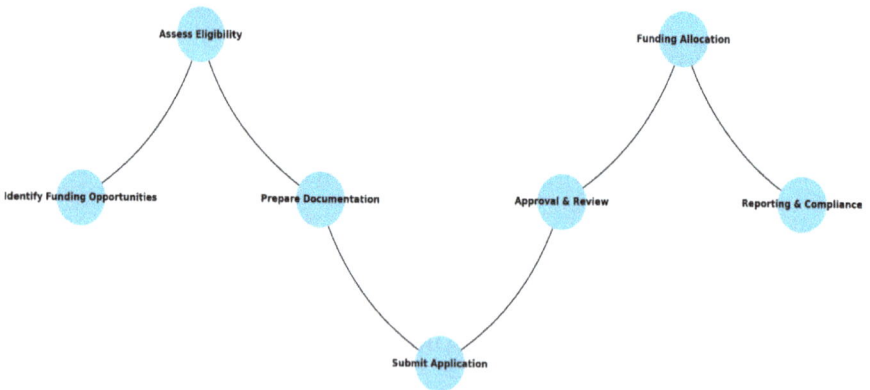

Key Insights:

- **Step-by-step clarity:** This structured approach ensures businesses understand the necessary actions for securing export financing.

- **Critical checkpoints:** The approval and review phase is crucial, as government agencies assess the viability of export projects.

- **Compliance matters:** Proper reporting and adherence to funding conditions ensure continued access to government support programs.

2.2 Tax Incentives for Exporting Businesses

1. **Duty Drawback Program:** Allows businesses to recover customs duties paid on imported goods used for export.

2. **Export Revenue Tax Benefits:** Some provinces offer tax incentives for businesses generating export income.

3. **Accelerated Investment Incentive:** Provides faster depreciation on capital investments for exporters.

3. Compliance and Regulatory Considerations

Navigating export regulations is critical to avoiding legal issues and maintaining international trade relationships.

3.1 Trade Compliance Requirements

1. **Customs Documentation:** Includes export permits, certificates of origin, and trade compliance reports.
2. **Sanctions and Embargoes:** Exporters must ensure compliance with international trade restrictions.
3. **Product Standards and Certification:** Countries often have unique technical requirements, such as CE marking in Europe or FDA approval in the U.S.

3.2 Intellectual Property Protection

1. **Patent Protection:** Ensuring inventions and proprietary technology are legally protected in international markets.

2. **Trademark Registration:** Protecting brand identity from infringement in foreign markets.

3. **Copyright Laws:** Safeguarding product designs, software, and digital content.

International Export Compliance Checklist

☑ Legal & Regulatory Compliance:

- Obtain necessary **export licenses and permits**.
- Ensure compliance with **customs regulations** in target countries.
- Check for **trade restrictions and sanctions**.

☑ Product Compliance & Standards:

- Verify that products meet **safety and quality standards** in target markets.
- Obtain necessary **certifications (ISO, FDA, CE, etc.)**.
- Ensure compliance with **packaging and labeling laws**.

☑ **Financial & Tax Compliance:**

- Understand **tariffs, duties, and tax implications** in different countries.

- Secure **export insurance** to mitigate financial risks.

- Set up proper **foreign currency exchange strategies**.

☑ **Logistics & Documentation:**

- Prepare **accurate invoices, bills of lading, and shipping documents**.

- Choose the right **Incoterms (FOB, CIF, EXW, etc.)** for shipments.

- Work with **reliable freight forwarders and customs brokers**.

☑ **Intellectual Property Protection:**

- Register **trademarks, patents, and copyrights** in international markets.

- Protect **sensitive business information** through legal agreements.

☑ **Market-Specific Compliance:**

- Understand **cultural and legal differences** in target countries.

- Ensure compliance with **advertising and consumer protection laws**.

- Develop a strategy for **dispute resolution and contract enforcement**.

Case Study: A Manufacturer's Success with Government Support

Company: ABC Tech Inc.

Industry: Advanced Manufacturing

Challenge: Expanding into European markets while navigating regulatory barriers.

Solution: The company leveraged CETA to eliminate tariffs, received CanExport funding for market research, and used EDC insurance to mitigate financial risks.

Outcome: Increased revenue by 35% within two years and established long-term contracts in Germany and France.

ABC Tech Inc.'s Revenue Growth After Leveraging Government Support

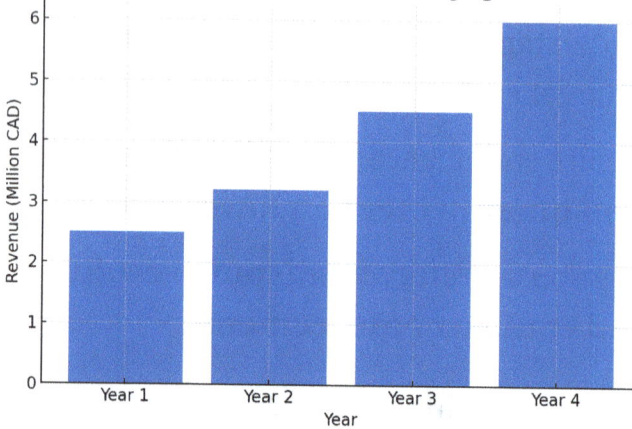

The bar graph illustrates the revenue growth of **ABC Tech Inc.** over a four-year period after the company utilized **government support programs** for export expansion. The steady upward trend in revenue highlights the **tangible impact of financial assistance, market development grants, and trade facilitation services** on a company's ability to scale in international markets.

Key Observations:

1. **Year 1: Initial Stage of Expansion**
   a. ABC Tech Inc. started with **$2.5 million** in revenue, reflecting its early efforts in export markets.

    b. At this stage, the company likely invested in **market research and compliance requirements** using government grants.

2. **Year 2: First Signs of Growth ($3.2M Revenue, ~28% Increase)**

    a. A notable jump in revenue occurred, indicating that **entry into international markets** started yielding results.

    b. This growth suggests **effective utilization of export financing** for production expansion.

3. **Year 3: Accelerated Expansion ($4.5M Revenue, ~40% Increase)**

    a. The company saw a substantial rise in revenue as it **expanded distribution networks and optimized supply chains**.

    b. This phase is where government support in **trade missions and global**

branding assistance likely played a critical role.

4. **Year 4: Market Maturity ($6.0M Revenue, ~33% Increase)**

    a. ABC Tech Inc. experienced **continued growth**, likely benefiting from **sustained export strategies, reduced production costs, and stable international demand.**

    b. This stage suggests that the company had gained a **strong foothold in key international markets** and was maximizing profits.

Conclusion & Strategic Insights:

The graph clearly demonstrates that government-backed export support programs can significantly **boost revenue growth** for Canadian manufacturers.

Businesses that leverage these resources effectively can experience **faster international market entry, improved operational efficiency, and**

long-term sustainability. For companies considering international expansion, investing in the right **funding, trade facilitation, and strategic partnerships** can yield significant financial benefits over time.

5. Actionable Strategy for Manufacturers

1. **Evaluate Trade Agreements**: Identify FTAs that provide tariff advantages in target markets.

2. **Apply for Government Funding**: Utilize CanExport and EDC financing to offset international expansion costs.

3. **Ensure Compliance**: Work with legal and regulatory experts to meet destination country requirements.

4. **Protect Intellectual Property**: Secure patents and trademarks before entering foreign markets.

5. **Develop a Risk Mitigation Plan**: Consider trade insurance and financial safeguards against potential market fluctuations.

Conclusion

Government policies, financial incentives, and compliance regulations significantly impact a manufacturer's ability to export successfully.

By leveraging trade agreements, funding opportunities, and ensuring compliance, Canadian manufacturers can achieve sustained international growth while mitigating risks.

In the next chapter, we will explore the role of digital transformation in export development, examining how new technologies and data-driven strategies can enhance global competitiveness.

CHAPTER 6
LEVERAGING E-COMMERCE FOR EXPORT DEVELOPMENT

Highlights of this Chapter

- ☑ Introduction
- ☑ The Role of E-Commerce in Export Development
- ☑ Key Benefits of E-Commerce for Exporting
- ☑ Choosing the Right E-Commerce Platform
- ☑ Popular E-Commerce Platforms for Canadian Exporters
- ☑ Digital Marketing Strategies for International Sales
- ☑ Effective Strategies
- ☑ Managing Logistics and Fulfillment in E-Commerce Exports
- ☑ Case Study: A Canadian Manufacturer's E-Commerce Export Success
- ☑ Challenges and Solutions

Introduction

E-commerce has revolutionized global trade, enabling businesses to reach international markets without the traditional barriers of physical expansion. Canadian manufacturers can significantly enhance their export development by leveraging e-commerce platforms, digital marketing, and streamlined logistics.

The Role of E-Commerce in Export Development

E-commerce facilitates seamless cross-border transactions by providing a digital storefront that can attract customers from around the world. With advancements in payment processing, logistics, and customer support, manufacturers can now expand into international markets more efficiently than ever before.

Key Benefits of E-Commerce for Exporting

- **Lower Market Entry Costs:** Unlike traditional brick-and-mortar expansion, e-commerce eliminates the need for physical presence in foreign markets.

- **24/7 Global Access:** Online stores operate continuously, catering to different time zones and increasing sales potential.

- **Data-Driven Insights:** Advanced analytics provide insights into customer behavior, enabling targeted marketing and improved decision-making.

- **Flexible Payment Solutions:** Digital payment options such as PayPal, Stripe, and cryptocurrency enhance accessibility for global customers.

- **Enhanced Customer Engagement:** E-commerce allows for direct interaction with international buyers through live chat, email support, and AI-driven recommendations.

Choosing the Right E-Commerce Platform

Selecting an appropriate platform is critical for success in global markets. The right platform should offer international reach, strong security features, and seamless integration with logistics providers.

Popular E-Commerce Platforms for Canadian Exporters

Platform	Features for Exporting
Shopify	Multi-currency support, localized marketing, global fulfillment solutions
Amazon Global	Established customer base, international shipping support
eBay	Easy international sales setup, automated tax and duty calculations
Alibaba	B2B focus, ideal for bulk orders and wholesale exports
WooCommerce	Customizable platform for businesses with existing websites

Digital Marketing Strategies for International Sales

E-commerce success is heavily reliant on digital marketing strategies that increase visibility and engagement in global markets.

Effective Strategies

- **Search Engine Optimization (SEO):** Optimizing product listings and website content for search engines in target countries.

- **Social Media Advertising:** Running paid campaigns on Facebook, Instagram, LinkedIn, and TikTok to target international customers.

- **Email Marketing:** Personalized email campaigns to nurture leads and retain customers.

- **Influencer Marketing:** Partnering with influencers in target markets to build brand credibility.

- **Localized Content:** Adapting marketing materials, including website language, product descriptions, and promotions, to resonate with local audiences.

Managing Logistics and Fulfillment in E-Commerce Exports

One of the biggest challenges in e-commerce exports is ensuring efficient order fulfillment. Partnering with third-party logistics (3PL) providers and using fulfillment centers in strategic locations can minimize shipping costs and delivery times.

Key Logistics Considerations

- **Warehousing Solutions:** Utilizing fulfillment centers in target markets to reduce shipping delays.
- **International Shipping Partners:** Choosing reliable carriers like FedEx, DHL, or UPS for cross-border shipments.
- **Customs & Duties Management:** Understanding regulations in each target country to ensure compliance and avoid unexpected costs.
- **Returns & Refund Policies:** Having clear policies in place to handle international returns smoothly.

Case Study: A Canadian Manufacturer's E-Commerce Export Success

Case: GreenTech Innovations A Vancouver-based manufacturer of eco-friendly home products leveraged Shopify and Amazon Global to expand into the European and Asian markets. By investing in multilingual customer support, targeted digital ads, and regional fulfillment centers, the company increased its international sales by 120% within two years.

Challenges and Solutions

While e-commerce provides immense export opportunities, manufacturers must navigate several challenges:

Challenge	Solution
High shipping costs	Partner with fulfillment centers and negotiate bulk shipping rates
Compliance with foreign regulations	Research international trade laws and work with legal consultants
Payment security concerns	Use trusted payment gateways and implement strong cybersecurity measures
Cultural and language barriers	Offer localized content and multilingual customer service

Future Trends in E-Commerce for Export Development

- **AI and Automation:** Chatbots and AI-driven customer service will enhance international engagement.

- **Blockchain for Secure Transactions:** Secure and transparent payment processing will increase trust in cross-border e-commerce.

- **Augmented Reality (AR):** AR shopping experiences will allow customers to preview products in a real-world setting before purchasing.

- **Sustainable E-Commerce Practices:** More businesses will adopt eco-friendly packaging and carbon-neutral shipping solutions.

Conclusion

E-commerce presents a transformative opportunity for Canadian manufacturers to develop their export businesses efficiently and cost-effectively. By selecting the right platforms, investing in digital marketing, and streamlining logistics, businesses can expand globally with fewer barriers. With continued advancements in technology and logistics, e-commerce is set to become the dominant force in international trade, making it an essential strategy for any manufacturer looking to grow beyond domestic markets.

CHAPTER 7

MASTERING EXPORT LOGISTICS AND SUPPLY CHAIN EFFICIENCY

Highlights of this Chapter

- ☑ Introduction
- ☑ Steps in Export Logistics
- ☑ Optimizing Supply Chain for Export Success
- ☑ Analytical Insights
- ☑ Case Study: A Canadian Manufacturer's Logistics Transformation
- ☑ How Blockchain Enhances Supply Chain Transparency and Reduces Fraud
- ☑ Global Shipping Routes and Key Logistics Hubs for Canadian Exporters

Introduction

Efficient logistics and a well-optimized supply chain are crucial for the success of any export business. Managing transportation, warehousing, and distribution efficiently can make a significant difference in cost savings, product quality, and customer satisfaction. In this chapter, we delve into strategies and best practices for Canadian manufacturers to master export logistics and enhance supply chain efficiency.

Understanding the Logistics Framework for Exporting

Export logistics involves multiple components, including transportation, customs clearance, warehousing, and distribution networks.

Canadian manufacturers must navigate domestic and international logistics requirements while ensuring compliance with trade regulations. Key considerations include:

- **Transportation Modes**: Choosing between air, sea, rail, and road transport depending on cost, delivery timelines, and product type.

- **Customs and Tariffs**: Understanding import/export duties, trade agreements, and necessary documentation.

- **Warehousing and Distribution**: Managing storage and ensuring timely delivery to global markets.

Steps in Export Logistics

1. **Product Ready** – The goods are manufactured or sourced, inspected for quality, and prepared for export.

2. **Packaging & Labeling** – Proper packaging and labeling are done according to the destination country's regulations and transportation requirements.

3. **Customs Documentation** – Essential export documents, such as invoices, certificates, and permits, are prepared for compliance.

4. **Shipping (Air, Sea, Rail, or Road)** – The exporter chooses the best transportation mode, and the goods are shipped.

5. **Customs Clearance** – The shipment undergoes customs checks in the importing country, where duties and taxes are assessed and paid.

6. **Warehousing & Distribution** – Once cleared, the goods are stored in warehouses or distribution centers near the destination market.

7. **Final Delivery** – The goods are transported to retailers, wholesalers, or direct customers, completing the export process.

Optimizing Supply Chain for Export Success

An efficient supply chain ensures that products reach international markets seamlessly. Strategies for optimizing supply chain operations include:

- **Supplier Management**: Establishing strong relationships with reliable suppliers to minimize disruptions.

- **Technology Integration**: Leveraging automation, AI, and IoT to track shipments and manage inventory.

- **Risk Mitigation**: Developing contingency plans for potential supply chain disruptions due to geopolitical events, trade restrictions, or natural disasters.

- **Sustainability in Logistics**: Reducing carbon footprint through eco-friendly packaging, optimizing transportation routes, and partnering with green logistics providers.

Cost-Effectiveness of Different Supply Chain Optimization Strategies

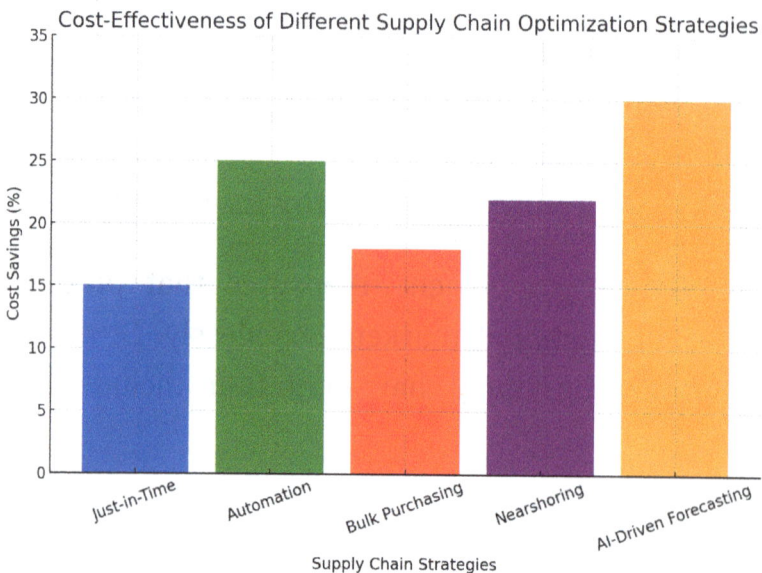

Bar chart titled "Cost-Effectiveness of Different Supply Chain Optimization Strategies" with y-axis "Cost Savings (%)" ranging from 0 to 35 and x-axis "Supply Chain Strategies": Just-in-Time (~15), Automation (~25), Bulk Purchasing (~18), Nearshoring (~22), AI-Driven Forecasting (~30).

Analytical Insights:

- **AI-Driven Forecasting (30% Cost Savings)**: The most effective strategy, as it optimizes demand prediction and minimizes excess inventory.

- **Automation (25% Cost Savings)**: Reduces labor costs and improves efficiency, making it a strong choice.

- **Nearshoring (22% Cost Savings)**: Brings production closer to the market, cutting transportation costs and supply chain risks.

- **Bulk Purchasing (18% Cost Savings)**: Reduces per-unit costs but may require significant storage capacity.

- **Just-in-Time (15% Cost Savings)**: Minimizes inventory holding costs but depends on reliable supply chains to prevent delays.

This comparison highlights how technology-driven strategies (AI and automation) tend to provide the highest cost savings, while traditional methods like bulk purchasing and JIT still offer efficiency gains but require careful execution.

Case Study: A Canadian Manufacturer's Logistics Transformation

ABC Manufacturing, a mid-sized Canadian exporter of industrial equipment, faced high shipping costs and frequent delays in international deliveries. By implementing a centralized distribution strategy and leveraging third-party logistics (3PL) providers, they reduced transit times by 30% and decreased costs by 20%. They also adopted a real-time tracking system, improving supply chain visibility and customer satisfaction.

The Role of Technology in Export Logistics

Technology plays a pivotal role in modernizing export logistics. Tools and solutions that enhance logistics management include:

- **Blockchain for Transparency**: Provides secure and transparent tracking of shipments.

- **Cloud-based Supply Chain Management (SCM) Software**: Enhances real-time decision-making and demand forecasting.

- **Robotic Process Automation (RPA)**: Reduces paperwork and streamlines customs clearance.

- **Artificial Intelligence (AI) for Route Optimization**: Minimizes delivery times and fuel costs.

How Blockchain Enhances Supply Chain Transparency and Reduces Fraud

1. Secure and Tamper-Proof Transaction Records

- Every transaction in the supply chain—from raw material sourcing to product delivery—is recorded on a **decentralized, immutable ledger**.

- This means **no single entity** can alter the records, reducing the risk of fraud or manipulation.

- Each block in the blockchain contains a **timestamp and a cryptographic hash** of the previous block, making it nearly impossible to alter historical data without detection.

2. Real-Time Tracking of Goods

- Blockchain allows businesses and consumers to track goods **in real-time** through **RFID tags, QR codes, or IoT sensors**.

- Every movement of a product (from production to shipment, distribution, and final delivery) is **recorded and accessible** by all stakeholders.

- If a shipment is delayed, lost, or altered, blockchain instantly **identifies where the issue occurred** and holds the responsible party accountable.

- For industries such as **pharmaceuticals and food safety**, tracking ensures that **expiration dates, storage conditions, and authenticity** are maintained throughout the supply chain.

3. Smart Contracts for Automated Compliance

- **Smart contracts** are self-executing contracts stored on a blockchain that automatically enforce agreements.

- For example, **a supplier will only receive payment once the agreed-upon shipment has been delivered in full and verified** by blockchain records.

- Smart contracts also help with **regulatory compliance**, ensuring that businesses meet international trade laws and product quality standards without manual paperwork.

- These contracts **reduce human errors, eliminate middlemen, and prevent fraudulent claims.**

4. Authentication of Product Origin

- Blockchain **tracks product origin and production history**, making it easy to verify the legitimacy of raw materials and manufactured goods.

- This is particularly valuable in industries such as:

  - **Luxury goods** (to prevent counterfeit designer products)

  - **Electronics** (to track ethical sourcing of materials like lithium and cobalt)

- ○ **Food & agriculture** (to ensure organic certification and fair-trade compliance)
- Consumers and businesses can scan a **blockchain-linked QR code** to verify a product's origin, ensuring that it was ethically and legally sourced.

5. Reduction of Counterfeit Goods Through Verifiable Data

- Counterfeit goods cost businesses billions of dollars every year, especially in industries like pharmaceuticals, fashion, and electronics.

- With blockchain, each product receives a **unique digital fingerprint**, such as:

  - ○ **RFID/NFC tags** that verify authenticity.

  - ○ **Cryptographic serial numbers** that prevent replication.

  - ○ **Digital certificates of authenticity** stored on the blockchain.

- Retailers, customs agencies, and consumers can instantly **validate whether a product is genuine** or tampered with.

Why It Matters?

1. Trust & Accountability

- Blockchain creates a **single source of truth**, eliminating the possibility of falsified data.

- Customers and business partners can **trust the information** about where a product came from, how it was handled, and whether it meets compliance standards.

2. Fraud Prevention

- Fraudulent practices such as **document forgery, illegal substitutions, and financial fraud** are significantly reduced.

- Manufacturers and retailers can ensure that **middlemen are not introducing fake or substandard products** into the supply chain.

3. Efficiency & Cost Reduction

- Blockchain **automates record-keeping, reducing administrative costs** and time spent on dispute resolution.

- By eliminating the need for **paper-based tracking systems**, businesses can **reduce overhead costs and improve logistics speed**.

4. Improved Consumer Confidence

- When consumers know a product is **authentic, ethically sourced, and tracked in real-time**, they are more likely to choose **trusted brands** over unknown competitors.

- Blockchain helps businesses **differentiate themselves** in the market by offering transparency as a competitive advantage.

Final Thoughts

Blockchain technology is transforming supply chain management by **reducing fraud, enhancing transparency, and building trust** across industries. By leveraging blockchain's ability to **track products in real-time, verify authenticity, and automate compliance**, businesses can create **more secure, cost-efficient, and ethical supply chains** for the future.

Future Trends in Global Logistics for Exporters

The future of global trade logistics is evolving, with advancements such as:

- **Autonomous Vehicles & Drones**: Increasing efficiency in last-mile delivery.

- **Green Logistics Innovations**: Focus on sustainability and reduced environmental impact.

- **Decentralized Warehousing**: Using smaller, strategically located warehouses for quicker delivery times.

- **5G Connectivity**: Enabling faster and more efficient communication within supply chain networks.

Global Shipping Routes and Key Logistics Hubs for Canadian Exporters

Efficient global shipping routes and logistics hubs play a crucial role in facilitating Canadian exports. Below is an overview of the most effective trade corridors, major ports, and logistics hubs that Canadian exporters rely on for smooth international trade.

1. Major Canadian Export Ports

Canada has several key ports that serve as the starting points for international shipping:

- **Port of Vancouver** (West Coast): Handles shipments to Asia-Pacific, including China, Japan, and South Korea.

- **Port of Montreal** (East Coast): A major gateway for exports to Europe and the U.S. Midwest.

- **Port of Halifax** (East Coast): Offers access to European and U.S. Atlantic markets with deep-water capabilities.

- **Port of Prince Rupert** (West Coast): The fastest route to Asia, reducing transit time compared to U.S. West Coast ports.

2. Key Global Trade Hubs

Once goods leave Canadian ports, they pass through major logistics hubs around the world:

- **Rotterdam, Netherlands**: Europe's largest port and a critical gateway for Canadian exports to the EU.

- **Shanghai, China**: The busiest container port, essential for Canadian goods entering Asian markets.

- **Singapore**: A strategic transshipment hub for Southeast Asia and beyond.

- **Los Angeles & Long Beach, USA**: Crucial for trade with the U.S. and Latin America.

3. *Major Shipping Routes*

Canadian exports travel along well-established global shipping lanes:

- **Trans-Pacific Route**: Connects the West Coast of Canada (Vancouver, Prince Rupert) to Asian markets such as China, Japan, and South Korea.

- **Trans-Atlantic Route**: Links Eastern Canadian ports (Montreal, Halifax) with Europe, including the U.K., Germany, and France.

- **North-South Route**: Serves trade between Canada and Latin America via U.S. ports or direct routes to Mexico and Brazil.

4. Logistics and Supply Chain Considerations

To optimize shipping efficiency, exporters must consider:

- **Freight consolidation**: Combining shipments to reduce costs.

- **Customs clearance efficiency**: Ensuring compliance with trade regulations to avoid delays.

- **Intermodal transportation**: Using rail and trucking services to connect ports with inland markets.

By leveraging these key ports, trade hubs, and shipping routes, Canadian exporters can ensure their goods reach international markets efficiently and cost-effectively. Let me know if you'd like additional details on any of these trade corridors!

Mastering export logistics and supply chain efficiency is critical for Canadian manufacturers looking to succeed in international markets. By leveraging technology, optimizing processes, and staying ahead of global trends, exporters can build a resilient and cost-effective supply chain that enhances competitiveness and ensures long-term growth.

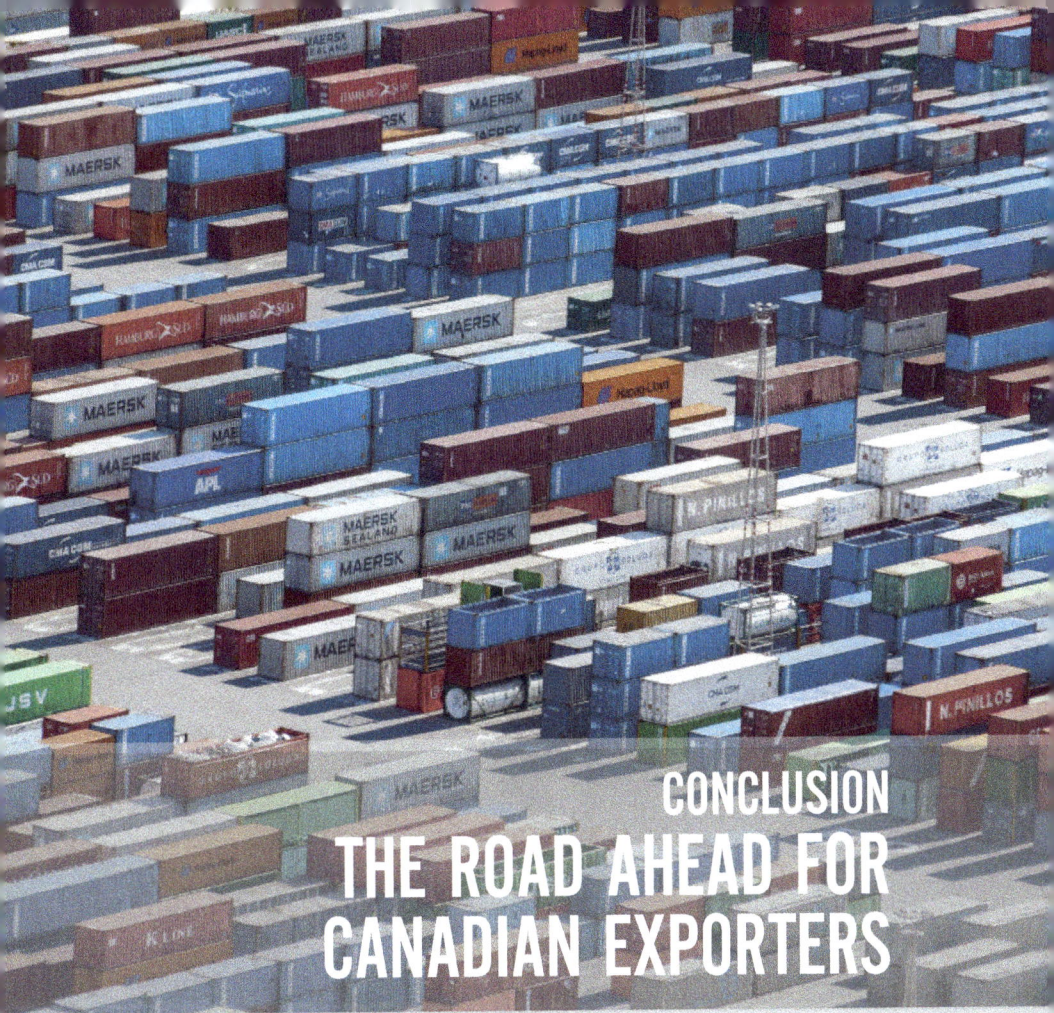

CONCLUSION
THE ROAD AHEAD FOR CANADIAN EXPORTERS

Highlights of this Chapter

☑ Key Takeaways for Canadian Exporters
☑ Building a Future of Sustainable Export Growth
☑ A Call to Action: Time to Act

As global markets evolve, Canadian manufacturers are presented with an unparalleled opportunity to expand their reach and achieve long-term success in international trade. Throughout this book, we have explored the key pillars of export development—ranging from market research and trade agreements to financing, logistics, technology adoption, and risk management. These are not just theoretical concepts but actionable strategies that can determine whether a company thrives or struggles in the global economy.

As we conclude, it is essential to recognize that **export success is not a destination but an ongoing journey**—one that requires adaptability, innovation, and strategic decision-making. The Canadian business landscape is rich with opportunities, but only those who take decisive action will reap the benefits.

Key Takeaways for Canadian Exporters

1. Strategic Market Entry Is the Foundation of Export Success

Entering a new market requires careful planning. **Blind expansion without research can be costly**, while a data-driven approach significantly increases success rates. Identifying the right markets, understanding consumer behavior, and complying with local regulations are essential for sustained export growth.

Actionable Insight: Utilize **Canada's free trade agreements (FTAs)** to gain competitive advantages in key global markets. The Comprehensive Economic and Trade Agreement (CETA) with the European Union, the Comprehensive and Progressive Agreement for Trans-Pacific Partnership (CPTPP), and the United States-Mexico-Canada Agreement (USMCA) open doors to billions of consumers with reduced trade barriers.

2. Government Support and Trade Organizations Are Untappe Resources

Many Canadian businesses **underutilize** the vast resources available to support exporters. Government agencies such as the **Trade Commissioner Service (TCS)** and **Export Development Canada (EDC)** provide grants, financing, and advisory services that reduce financial risks and facilitate international expansion.

Actionable Insight: Businesses should develop a **government partnership strategy**—leveraging trade missions, securing funding from export programs, and attending international trade expos with Canadian delegations to establish global connections.

3. Supply Chain Resilience and Optimization Define Long-Term Success

The past decade has proven that **supply chains can make or break an export strategy.** The COVID-19 pandemic, geopolitical tensions, and logistical bottlenecks have highlighted the **importance of resilience** in international trade.

Businesses must optimize supply chains by incorporating **regional suppliers, digital tracking systems, and alternative shipping routes** to avoid disruptions.

Actionable Insight: Consider **nearshoring** (partnering with suppliers in closer markets) and **diversifying logistics providers** to mitigate risks. Additionally, leveraging technologies such as **AI-driven demand forecasting** can help optimize inventory and avoid over-reliance on single suppliers.

4. Digital Trade and Innovation Are Reshaping the Export Landscape

Traditional export models are becoming obsolete in the face of **e-commerce, digital marketplaces, and AI-driven global sales strategies**. Businesses that integrate digital platforms can **significantly reduce market entry barriers** and gain access to customers worldwide.

Actionable Insight: Invest in **multilingual e-commerce websites**, partner with global B2B platforms like **Alibaba and Amazon Global**, and implement AI-driven marketing analytics to tailor export strategies. Digital transformation is no longer optional—it is a necessity for long-term export success.

5. Risk Management Is Crucial in an Uncertain Global Economy

Global trade comes with **inherent risks**—currency fluctuations, trade wars, regulatory changes, and political instability can disrupt business operations. Companies that **proactively assess risks** and develop mitigation strategies will be in a stronger position to withstand challenges.

Actionable Insight: Businesses should secure **export credit insurance**, use **hedging strategies for currency fluctuations**, and establish **multi-market diversification plans** to spread risk across different regions rather than relying on a single export destination.

Building a Future of Sustainable Export Growth

Exporting is not just about selling products abroad—it is about **building long-term global business relationships, enhancing brand reputation,**

and driving economic growth. Canadian manufacturers must **embrace a global mindset** while maintaining high standards in **quality, innovation, and sustainability**.

Adapting to Evolving Trade Trends: Global trade policies, sustainability regulations, and consumer preferences are **constantly changing**. Companies must **stay informed and flexible**—continuously updating strategies based on emerging trends such as carbon-neutral shipping, digital trade compliance, and supply chain decarbonization.

Developing Long-Term Partnerships: Export success is often **rooted in strong relationships** with **international distributors, suppliers, and trade organizations**. Businesses should actively seek **joint ventures, strategic alliances, and co-branding opportunities** to strengthen their global presence.

Commitment to Continuous Learning: The most successful exporters **never stop learning**. Whether it is attending trade summits, engaging in government-led training programs, or adopting new technologies, continuous improvement is the key to maintaining a **competitive advantage in global markets**.

A Call to Action: Time to Act

The knowledge and strategies outlined in this book are only valuable if put into practice. **Now is the time to act.**

- Conduct an internal export readiness assessment—identify strengths and areas for improvement.

- Research potential target markets and align them with your product's value proposition.

- Connect with government trade agencies and secure financial support for international expansion.

- Optimize your supply chain and logistics to increase cost efficiency.

- Leverage digital tools and e-commerce platforms to streamline export operations.

- Build relationships with **global trade partners, distributors, and strategic allies**.

- Stay updated on trade agreements and global economic shifts to adjust your export strategies accordingly.

Canadian manufacturers have a unique opportunity to become global leaders. By embracing innovation, leveraging government support, and developing **resilient, forward-thinking export strategies**, they can **achieve sustained growth in the international marketplace**.

The world is waiting—**it's time to take your business beyond borders.**

ABOUT THE AUTHOR

Peyman is a business consultant, finance and real estate professional, and entrepreneur with extensive experience in helping businesses grow and expand into new markets. Over the years, he has worked closely with business owners, investors, and manufacturers to develop strategic plans that drive success.

The inspiration for this book came during a time of economic uncertainty when the tariff war between Canada and the United States placed immense pressure on Canadian manufacturers. Witnessing firsthand the struggles of businesses that relied heavily on the U.S. market, Peyman realized that the best path forward was to explore new global opportunities. He dedicated himself to researching and developing strategies that would help Canadian businesses thrive beyond North America.

Peyman has extensive hands-on experience in international trade, having owned and operated an international trading company in Hong Kong and engaged in global commerce in Dubai for several years. His firsthand knowledge of international markets and trade logistics provides valuable insights for businesses looking to expand globally and made him a credential trade and export advisor to manufacturers.

With a deep passion for international trade and a strong belief in the power of economic diversification, Peyman wrote this book as a practical guide for manufacturers and exporters looking to expand their reach. His insights are based on real-world challenges and proven solutions, making this book an essential resource for anyone looking to navigate the complexities of global trade successfully.

email:

info@druckerpro.com

Website:

https://www.druckerpro.com

https://peymanchalabi.ca

www.ingramcontent.com/pod-product-compliance
Lightning Source LLC
Chambersburg PA
CBHW071434210326
41597CB00020B/3787